THE BERKSHIRES

THE BERKSHIRES

Bill Binzen

BERKSHIRE HOUSE PUBLISHERS
Stockbridge, Massachusetts

First edition published in 1986 by Skyline Press (Toronto) and in 1989 by Globe Pequot Press. Present revised edition published in 1995 by Berkshire House Publishers.

Original design by Fortunato Agliagoro. Revised pages designed by Jane McWhorter. Production services by Ripinsky & Co., Connecticut.

Library of Congress Cataloging-in-Publication Data
Binzen, Bill
     The Berkshires / Bill Binzen.
         p.   cm.
     ISBN 0-936399-67-8
      1. Berkshire Hills (Mass.)—Pictorial Works. I. Title
  F72.B5B69   1995
  974.4'1—dc20   94-24549
                                                       CIP

ISBN: 0-936399-67-8

10 9 8 7 6 5 4 3 2 1

Printed in Singapore

INTRODUCTION

When I opened my mail one day a few years ago and read a letter which suggested the possibility of my doing a book of photographs on the Berkshires, I couldn't have been more intrigued. The Berkshires are, after all, just down the road and they are among my favorite places in all the world—and certainly the place I know best and have the greatest feeling for. The prospect of meandering around the Berkshires over the course of a year, exploring the villages and country roads and seeing what the people are up to filled me with delight.

An encyclopedia would tell us that the Berkshires are a part of the Appalachian system and a continuation of the Green Mountains of Vermont. It is a rolling highland of long, wooded ridges fairly uniform in height, broken and intersected by valleys. With its numerous lakes and overall appearance, it is often compared with the English lake country.

The area known as the Berkshires includes Berkshire County—the westernmost county in Massachusetts. The Berkshires do not have a precise border that I know of, so I beg to be excused if I seem to have gone too far, or not far enough, in certain directions. To the north I stopped at the Vermont border and to the west at the New York line. While the countryside beyond these borders is very lovely indeed, each seems to me to have a personality of its own, somewhat removed from that of the Berkshires. To the east I followed a rather jagged line not actually drawn on a map but determined only by intuition. To the south I included the Litchfield Hills in the northwest corner of Connecticut, which are geographically part of the Berkshires.

There is a wonderful balance in the natural world of the Berkshires. The mountains are not too high but high enough; the valleys are not too deep but deep enough; the lakes are not too big but big enough. They all seem to work together in perfect harmony.

It's a fact that there are no big booming spectacles in the Berkshires—nothing absolutely bowls you over. Rather there is a succession of little things that attract your attention and make you feel enriched for having observed them. It may be the line of the hilltops above the trees, or the way a stream meanders through a meadow.

There can't be many places in the world where the flow of the seasons is as interesting and as rewarding to the eye as in the Berkshires. Each season has a distinct personality and each seems to relish expressing itself to the fullest.

Complementing the natural world, but equally as interesting, are sights that take us back to Colonial times; old stone fences, the village greens, the winding roads, the wonderful churches, the fields cleared out of the woods, the ancient gravestones—all are reminders of the past in a way that is both graphic and emotional.

But, of course, there is more to the Berkshires than scenery and history. There are the people today who farm the land, tend the shops, teach the children and do the thousand and one other things that occupy people nearly everywhere. Some of these folks have roots going back generations, some have just moved in, but most I've met seem to feel that they wouldn't ever want to live any place else and, after all, that's the way it should be!

BILL BINZEN

1 There are some who would say that, in its own quiet way, there is no place on earth more pleasant than the Berkshires.

2 There is much to suggest that those who came before us were very capable of creating beauty in their own right, as this church spire in Litchfield, Connecticut would suggest.

3 (*right*) The Berkshires are still very rural, as they were in days gone by. This corn field is in Ashley Falls, Massachusetts.

4 After a long Berkshire winter what could be more inviting than the spring flowers at the Berkshire Botanical Garden in Stockbridge, Massachusetts?

5 *(right)* From 1902–12 Edith Wharton lived at The Mount, the estate she built at Lenox, Massachusetts which is now open to visitors. Some of her best known novels, including *Ethan Frome*, were written during this period.

6 It's pretty hard to drive very far in the Berkshires without passing an antique shop. This one is in Sheffield, Massachusetts.

7 (*right*) White horse and red barn in Sheffield.

8   Ever since 1928, the town band of Salisbury, Connecticut, seen here playing at the Town Grove, has been making some of the most rousing music one could hope to hear.

9   *(right)* Few elms still thrive in the Berkshires, but some that remain are majestic — all the more so for being flanked by spring apple blossoms.

10 The mills of Rising Paper (now a division of the Fox River Paper Company) in Housatonic, Massachusetts have been making fine paper on this spot since 1900.

11 *(right)* Looking down on Tyringham, Massachusetts from the west one can easily imagine that the scene hasn't changed much in a century or more.

12 (*left*) The colors of spring can be as subtle as the colors of autumn are flamboyant.

13 The Berkshires are well endowed with old graveyards such as this one in Sharon, Connecticut. Often their gravestones hark back to the earliest days of Colonial settlement.

14 The Church on the Hill in Lenox, Massachusetts looks down benevolently upon those heading north out of the village. This Congregational Church was built in 1805.

15 (*right*) This eye-catching Victorian house sits along a quiet side street in Hinsdale, Massachusetts.

16 What better way to spend a sunny afternoon in July than on the porch of the Red Lion Inn in Stockbridge, Massachusetts?

17 A bench along a gentle stretch of the
Housatonic River invites the spirit to linger.

18 (*left*) A Kent School crew in Kent, Connecticut about to take to the Housatonic River for a race on a Saturday in May.

19 Visiting Morris Dancers do some fancy stepping by the green in Ashley Falls, Massachusetts. They wear bells 'to ward off evil spirits.'

20 Throughout the Berkshires volunteer firemen perform invaluable service to their communities. Here a raw recruit takes the wheel.

21 *(right)* A hot property under the gavel at a country auction in Richmond, Massachusetts.

22 Gloriosa daisies peek over the fence at passersby along a street in Lenox, Massachusetts.

23 (*right*) A serpentine line of waiting school buses suggests the winding country lanes along which children are driven to school in the Berkshires.

24 A Civil War statue catches the late afternoon sun as it gazes across North Adams, Massachusetts and towards the west.

25   The 127-foot spire of the First Congregational Church in Lee, Massachusetts, the tallest free-standing wooden structure in America, rises over buildings along the main street.

26 The Pittsfield Fourth of July Parade has become popular nationally
thanks to television — but nothing beats being right on the spot.

27 The Shed at Tanglewood in Lenox, Massachusetts is not the only place on the grounds where great music is heard. Here, an audience is enjoying an *al fresco* performance during *Tanglewood on Parade* late in August.

28 *(left)* Norman Rockwell's Stockbridge studio now sits on a beautiful knoll overlooking the Housatonic River, on the grounds of the new museum devoted to his work.

29 When it comes to ivy-covered walls Williams College in Williamstown, Massachusetts can certainly compete with the best of them.

30 Vintage automobiles and an enthusiastic audience gather annually at Chesterwood, a National Trust property and the former home of famed sculptor Daniel Chester French, in Stockbridge, Massachusetts.

31 *(right)* A working farm, one of a diminishing but beloved number, sits tranquilly on the rolling hills near Richmond, Massachusetts.

32 On certain days the clouds over the Berkshires seem determined to steal the scene from whatever lies below.

33 (*right*) A fine Victorian house resides in uncrowded splendor in Cheshire, Massachusetts.

34 The front door of the Lanesborough Episcopal Church in Lanesborough, Massachusetts seems at one with the falling snow.

35 (*right*) Snow resting on boughs and twigs makes a fine filigree along a road near Richmond, Massachusetts.

36 (left) The venerable sport of angling snags a new enthusiast, here trying his luck on a Berkshire stream.

37 A young apprentice helps to ready the sets for a performance at the Berkshire Theatre Festival in Stockbridge, Massachusetts, a summer hit that has been running since 1928.

38 *(left)* A simple arch seems to be extending an invitation into someone's secret garden.

39 A train pulls into the historic Canaan Union Station in Canaan, Connecticut. Formerly dilapidated, this line now carries as many as forty freight trains per week.

40 *(left)* Glamorous new Seiji Ozawa Hall is now Tanglewood's home to recitals, chamber concerts, and popular Friday-evening prelude concerts in Lenox, Massachusetts.

41 Young student dancers at Jacob's Pillow in Becket, Massachusetts carry their exuberance from practice in the studio straight into the out-of-doors.

42 A church in Otis, Massachusetts finds itself in the spotlight of the late afternoon sun.

43 (*right*) Pontoosuc Lake at Pittsfield, Massachusetts is a pleasant sight on a warm summer's day.

44 (*left*) Nothing suggests the arrival of summer more poetically than the blooming of the mountain laurel.

45 Life is still quiet and gracious among the handsome old houses of Litchfield, Connecticut.

46 (*left*) Winter doesn't like to be predictable. On occasion, it may come early and dust the foliage with powdered sugar.

47 A farm in the countryside above Great Barrington, Massachusetts patiently waits for spring.

48 In Housatonic, Massachusetts a wood sculptor works on a giant rocking horse of carved red oak. When completed it will represent eighteen months worth of work.

49 The Berkshires are generously endowed with artists and craftsmen. In Monterey, Massachusetts a potter goes about the work at hand.

IN
memory of
DEACON·NATHANIEL
BUELL.
who Departed this life the 27th
day of November. 1808.
in 75th year of
his age.

Lord I commit my Soul to the
Accept the sacred trust.
Receive part of me.
And Sleeping dust
Till morning come.

50 Veterans from battles of long ago are touchingly remembered in the graveyards of the Berkshires.

51 (*right*) On days like this it must be hard to concentrate on the books at Williams College in Williamstown, Massachusetts.

52   Rooting for the home team Class A Mets at Wahconah Park, Pittsfield, Massachusetts.

53   The canoes of latter-day voyageurs, resting along the Housatonic River
in Ashley Falls, Massachusetts.

54 (*left*) A farmer's work is never done. There is always one more cow to milk or a fence to mend.

55 These Black Angus cattle must be wondering where all that nice grass disappeared to overnight.

56 This hand-painted sign, standing at a strategic corner of the village green
in Norfolk, Connecticut, has been pointing innumerable travelers to their
destinations for some 150 years.

57 Spruced up Victorian houses along Church Street in North Adams, Massachusetts face today with cheerful facades. At one point the wrecking ball was just days away from demolishing them.

58   The oldest covered bridge in Massachusetts, a beloved treasure of Sheffield, Massachusetts, was tragically destroyed by fire in July 1994.

59   *(right)* A serene day, gentle mounts — the best way to see the byways of the Berkshires.

60　*(left)* Berkshire farmers of a few generations back would be somewhat alarmed to see their fields in autumn dotted with curious giant jellyrolls such as these.

61　Herman Melville bought this house in Pittsfield, Massachusetts in 1850. He named it 'Arrowhead' and it was here that he wrote *Moby Dick*. Today it is the home of the Berkshire County Historical Society and is open to visitors from May through October.

62 (*left*) When it's 10 above zero and the wind is blowing one can only hope that there will be a cozy fire at the end of the road.

63 There is something quite moving about the first snow of winter. Here it is in Great Barrington, Massachusetts.

64 A Williams College student turns her back on Edgar
Degas' *Little Dancer* to study a painting by Renoir at the
Clark Art Institute in Williamstown, Massachusetts.

65 Berkshire history is never better remembered that when it is reenacted, as here by members of the 25th Continental Regiment from Southampton, Massachusetts at an encampment at Bartholomew's Cobble in Ashley Falls, Massachusetts.

66   *(left)* Picnickers on the lawns of the Berkshire School in Sheffield, Massachusetts anticipate a summer performance by members of the Berkshire Choral Institute.

67   Many a rousing hockey game has taken place down through the years on Factory Pond in Lakeville, Connecticut.

68 In the country fetching the mail is a certain way of getting some fresh air. These mail boxes are awaiting their daily delivery in Falls Village, Connecticut.

69 (*right*) Wintry hedges serve as splendid ramparts for this Stockbridge, Massachusetts residence.

70 *(left)* On this hillside high above the Stockbridge Bowl stood 'Shadowbrook,' the grandest of all the Berkshire 'Cottages.' Time and a disastrous fire swept the house away, but the panorama endures.

71 'Naumkeag', the many-gabled summer mansion designed by Stanford White in Stockbridge, Massachusetts was built in 1886 for Ambassador and Mrs. Joseph Hodges Choate.

72 A lone Indian on the Mohawk Trail, west of Charlemont, Massachusetts, reflects on the changes time has wrought on his meandering pathway.

73 (right) On occasion, when you have to get there in a hurry, you can't do much better than the Mass. Pike which flows effortlessly across the Berkshires from east to west.

74 Citizens Hall in Interlaken, once the public school and town meeting hall, is now home to the lively Interlaken School of Art.

75 *(right)* This cluster in Sharon, Connecticut refutes the notion that all Berkshire barns must be red.

76 One could do worse in the summertime than live in a white clapboard house surrounded by a garden of flowers. This scene is in South Williamstown, Massachusetts.

77 (*right*) A street in South Egremont, Massachusetts reflects a magic moment in early October when the leaves are at their most resplendent.

78 Every summer visitors enjoy the beautiful rose gardens and land-scaped grounds of 'Naumkeag' in Stockbridge, Massachusetts.

79 (right) The Hancock Shaker Village with its famous round barn is located a short distance west of Pittsfield, Massachusetts. It was first settled in 1780 but after the departure of the last two Shakers in 1960 it became a public museum.

80 Three small members of the Hutterian Brothers, a religious community in Norfolk, Connecticut, get a ride in their father's wheelbarrow.

81 *(right)* A peaceful tour over the valley of the Housatonic, looking north toward Massachusetts.

82 *(left)* Springtime patterns follow nature's slope across a field in Sheffield, Massachusetts.

83 Columns and spires complement the green hills surrounding the Salisbury School in Salisbury, Connecticut.

84 The covered bridge in West Cornwall, Connecticut was built of native oak. The men who built it could not have visualized in 1837 the outlandish vehicles that cross it today.

85 (*right*) These red silos in Southfield, Massachusetts have to sport fresh paint to compete with the autumn colors all around them.

86 (*left*) The canoe is as much a native of Berkshire lakes as the fish who swim in their sparkling waters.

87 Certain characters appear in the Berkshire countryside every year along about mid-October. This one popped up in West Cornwall, Connecticut.

88 Three cows, unaware of their importance to the economic well-being of the Berkshires, bask in the warmth of the late autumn sun.

89 (*right*) A solitary tree on the horizon appears as a lone actor on the Berkshire stage.

90 Some evenings, as the sun prepares to dip behind the
Berkshire hills, there comes a stillness when man and
nature are at one.